The Cards We Hold

Payal Sareen

BookLeaf
Publishing

India | USA | UK

Presentation by *BookLeaf Publishing*

Web: www.bookleafpub.com

E-mail: info@bookleafpub.com

ISBN: 978-93-5744-764-5

First edition 2022

DEDICATION

For N-

Without you I would not have taken half the leaps I have. Thank you for allowing me to be myself and inspiring me to be so much more.

PREFACE

Dear Reader,

I've spent so long in my mind sometimes I can't find the words to say. Poetry has helped me make sense of my feelings and shown me how much can be said in a few words. It is not measured in impeccable technique or perfect grammar. It allows you to just exist without expectation.

If there is anything I hope you take away from this book it is that life is a beautiful experience if you allow it to be. There will be highs and lows but how you feel in those moments is up to you. At the end of the day, only you can decide if you lived a life worth living.

The Cards We Hold was made to help others find comfort in the experiences we share. It is a reminder that you hold your power. Give yourself the space to flourish and don't be afraid of the unknown. To grow we must push ourselves to jump when we feel the most fear and in those moments I hope you cherish the words I have written. The journey to your best self is a path you must walk alone, so pick up any piece of wisdom you can along the way and keep going.

With Love,
Payal

A Second Chance

I beg the divine for revelation,
plead for it to light a spark.
Longing for steady electricity once again.
I'm sick of fleeting feelings.

Anything I am,
becoming one with me.
Filling my soul with
desire.
Desire to live,
to love,
to learn,
all over again.

Remind me of all the reasons I want to stay
because there are oh so many.
Fill aspiration back into my heart.
I want to fall once again.
Fall in love with my dreams
and be present enough to feel it all.

The Presence of Rain

Rain is always in a hustle,
always has somewhere to be
with not enough time.

Occupying my days for weeks on end,
rain can never make up its mind.

Rain calls for me
during quiet nights and full moons.
Whistling my name in ciphered symphonies,
creating its own ensemble
in hopes I will join the fun.

Rain is the lover I can't shake.
Pooling around my feet
submerging me in its presence,
I sink into rain's desires.

But, rain sticks by me.
When I tell it to leave,
rain stays.

I beg rain for sunshine.
Clinging to my body
I tell rain
I need space.

Rain replies,
"no."

An Unsigned Love Letter

I crave a love so deep
the ocean's depth can't compare.
A love so pure
cupid can't look away.

Our mouths don't need to speak a word
for our eyes to have a conversation.
A partner
that never leaves my side
because our souls
are intertwined with fire.

Our bond so strong
the lions roar in approval.
There is no question this is love.

Symphonies began to play
when I look into your eyes.
The windows to your soul.

And our souls remind us
we have been here before.

And in every life after this,
we will find our way back.

Angel

My generous angel,
my number one supporter.
You have helped shape my world,
revealing to me the finest parts of life.

On the days we talk for hours
you tell me about your childhood,
you tell me about life back home.
Paint a picture so vivid,
I want to go back with you.

On the days we sit in silence,
there is no pressure to fill the time.
Your company is my blessing.
Your thoughts,
my reward.

Broken Promises

Are we friends?
Because I don't feel treated as one.
I don't enjoy your rude remarks
and trust me there are many.

Enduring this because we're "besties" doesn't
seem worth it anymore.
It feels more like a task.
Walking on a tightrope to keep you happy,
because your happiness has always been worth
more than mine.

Your frustration towards me comes from your
inability to cope.
It's always my fault.
I'm always wrong.
So I have to make it right.

Do I deserve this?
I give you more than I give myself.
Let myself break piece by piece,
To build you up when you're feeling down.

There is no equal balance here.
No winning this game.

You're victorious.
And standing beneath you,
Me.

I sacrifice for you and that's the truth.

I Still See You

I despise the part of me who sees glimpses of
you in others.
How cruel of me to strip them of their identity,
to make them fit
into my delusional fantasy.

The Real Her

I often feel diminished,
reduced to the parts that only others see.
I don't fit into a box,
yet I feel there's something missing of me.

I don't want to be known by my
accomplishments,
or my mistakes.
I want to give out love the way it was given to
me,
and be known for my heart.

My heart that pours it's all into everything.
Passion integrated into the works I have created.

My heart that chooses to love harder
even after being wounded so many times.

And my heart that wants to treat with you
compassion
because I know how hard these years have been.

I want it to be known,
I am more than the sum of my parts.
I see you for who you are,
and I hope that you now see me.

When Night Comes

Running through the streets
with shackles on our feet.

We laugh in the night
and hope we get home before light.

Feeling lost but free,
between wildflowers and symphonies.

Who cares when the world is asleep?
Steady making promises we know we won't
keep.

Till tomorrow comes
we will be just fine.

And pretend that nothing happened,
late last night.

Stuck In My Ways

I spend my nights
thinking of the ways you find your way back to
me.
Until I remember,
that's not how it should be.
And in my mind
I wonder what I'm waiting for.
But I'm too ashamed to admit it's you.
How silly of me to give you myself
and expect your love in return.

Destiny

There have been many times
I wondered if it was me.
If I had destiny beat.
Maybe destiny wasn't aware of my fast walk
or how I avoided eye contact like it was the
plague.
Did destiny know about my resting bitch face?
I wondered,
if I had evaded your glance every time we
passed.
Turned the corner right as you did.
Or if I had just taken a leap of faith,
said something,
anything.
If maybe you could have been the one.
Me and destiny spent days running in circles
playing these same games.
But destiny was always one step ahead.
And every time I tried to catch up,
destiny slipped away.
I told myself destiny just has other plans.
But then again,
what do I know about destiny?

Never Lasting Moment

In the divide between space and time
I watch the world from a distance.
I search for peace,
a nostalgic feeling
with an irreplaceable embrace.

Yearning for the past while trying to live in the
present.
Memories replaying in my head.
I feel still for a moment,
a stillness that gives me perspective.
I feel lighter
as I return to my body.

Unaffected by everything around me,
I forget the world continues spinning.
In that moment
I pray time stops.
To hold on to this feeling
For just one more second.

An Ode to My Midnight Wanderer

I see you every night in my dreams.
You've figured out how to craft my perfect
reality.
You are the reason I lay around in bed till noon,
and are the cause of my bittersweet feelings.
But still.
I wake up every morning
in eager anticipation of returning to your arms.
It is the only time I truly get to hold you.
In return you sing me soft lullabies
and request that I stay.
Now I think you're catching on
because the goodbyes are getting harder,
and our time together feeling shorter.
And I don't know how much longer I can keep
saying,
I can't.

Forever

I have dreams of laying by your side

on this swaying hammock.

The only place where we are a perfect fit.

As we go back and forth,

the Arizona sun settles down for the night,

and I dig my face deeper into your chest.

I fall asleep.

Wishing we stay like this forever.

I Pick Me

Sometimes I despised the confident version of
myself.
She knew her worth.
She knew never to settle and only allow the best.
The version of me that never allowed herself to
look desperate.
Never texted old exes and never gave up a part
of herself for anyone else.
She made my life difficult sometimes.
She didn't know how to bend to a lover's
desires.
Never felt security in the words they told her.
And never wanted help from anyone.

But that version of me is also insecure.
Never texted old exes because she's scared they
won't text back.
Never gave up a part of herself because she's
always been too selfish to compromise.
Never felt security because she has been
betrayed one too many times.
And never asked for help because she has
forgotten how.

These versions of us never cease to exist.
In the end we must find a way to live with both.

18

Home

Home is where my happiness resides. But home has many names and even more locations. I haven't met every version of home and I slowly grow impatient. Little compares to the comfort. The warm embrace that reminds me it's okay to breathe. A haven of peace built by bricks of compassion. Like a secret hidden in a safe, this fortress is impenetrable. Home is meals cooked by grandma and scary movies at night. Where we spent hours playing barbies and days making puzzles. As we get older, home changes. Maybe home is now a foreign city you have claimed as your own. Or maybe home is now the boy who lives a couple doors down. But every version of home has made a place in my heart. And when I now think about home, I think of your arms.

Ignorance is Bliss

I lay beside her
and ask her what falling in love is like.
Something I've only dreamed of.

She begins to tell me.
Scared of the consequences,
I stop listening.
Maybe it's best I don't know.

Complications

Living under the same roof
I've learnt how to distract myself.
As mother's sharp tongue
jabs at father's insecurities.
Constantly reminding him of his shortcomings.
He chooses to return with a witty smackdown.
Day after day,
I have grown tired of the same routine.
Our kitchen is the battlefield
and insults are thrown like frisbees.
I quickly learn frisbees is a better substitution,
because this broken glass is still cluttering the
floor.
I guess trying to mend a broken marriage
starts with some destruction.

On Days I Want to Disappear

There are days I want to disappear.
Throw on a hat and hide behind my hair.
I don't want to make pointless conversations..
I want to just exist.

There are weeks where I don't feel like talking.
Most of that time spent thinking of what I would
say.
I have become my own best friend
and my favourite companion.

Now weeks turn into months
and I have forgotten faces.
I barely check my phone,
there is no one on the other side waiting.

Years spent asking myself the same questions.
Why am I here?
What is my purpose?
The same questions I have been trying to find
answers to
all

this
time.

Loving You From a Distance

I know when they tell me
distance makes the heart grow fonder,
they are not lying.

I keep telling you I can do this anymore.
You have left a permanent imprint.
And every day away for you
is slowly killing me.

You Will Not Be Softer.

You will not be softer. On days you are called a raging bitch. On days you are the dog barking orders. On days you are the uptight organized freak. You will not be softer. They will tell you that you are acting irrational. They will tell you that you are over-emotional. They will tell you that you didn't deserve it. On those days you tell them you will not be softer. You will walk with confidence guiding your every stride and faith by your side. You will not be spoken over. You will not be taken for granted. And you will not take their shit. For you have not come this far to be disregarded. For others to reduce you to your past selves. You have fought every day for respect. And you have damn well earned it. So, you will not be goddam soft now. Not now, not ever. You have earned this privilege.

Inner Child

My heart aches for the old me.
I wish I could tell her
how great we're doing now.
And apologize for all the ways
I let her down.

I would tell her
I'm sorry I allowed you to get hurt.
For believing other's opinions,
mattered more than mine.
Coercing you into thinking you weren't good
enough for me,
when you woke up every day trying your best to
succeed.
Most of all,
I'm sorry I let you be treated
as if u didn't matter.
I realize now
all the ways I have hurt you.

It hurts to see how I deceived you.
Tried to trick you into thinking that was
happiness.
You deserved so much more.
So when I look back and my heart aches for you

I can't help but feel guilty.

We have come so far,
conquered dreams
day by day.
Fought so hard for happiness
that it never leaves.
Bad days don't scare me
because I know we are not the same anymore.

So, I thank you for everything you went through.
You are the reason I stand strong.
You are the foundation that my feet have finally
felt ease on.
Grounding me to this earth,
reminding me
you still lay deep within me.

I know this apology is not enough,
but I will try again tomorrow.
I have now become the parent
to my inner child.

ACKNOWLEDGEMENT

First, I would like to thank anyone who has taken the time to read this book and given me a chance to share this experience with you. Without you I would have nothing more than scattered thoughts and notebooks filled with poetry no one would have ever read. I am truly grateful for your time and hope you have also found the courage to dream big.

Thank you to my family for pushing me towards new opportunities and supporting me through the new ventures of my life. You have shown me unconditional love and have brought me laughter in the purest form.

To my dearest friends, Kaitlyn, Priya, and Jessel. For being with me through the toughest of times. You have been a constant light in my life and I can't imagine being where I am without you. Our love knows no boundaries and in my darkest times, it is the reason I keep going.

To my favourite teacher, Jennifer Twigg. For reminding me that my hard work will never go unnoticed. You have given me the courage to pursue countless dreams and have never let me down. Thank you for your guidance and acceptance.

Lastly, to anyone who has come into my life, whether it be for a moment or a lifetime. You have inspired these poems and given me the gift of your presence. I believe we were destined to meet and I hope I have made an impact on you, the way you have on me.

-Payal

www.ingramcontent.com/pod-product-compliance
Lightning Source LLC
LaVergne TN
LVHW010943200726
843509LV00013B/2274